Bodily Salute

Elena Ilkova

BookLeaf
Publishing

Presentation by *BookLeaf Publishing*

Web: www.bookleafpub.com

E-mail: info@bookleafpub.com

ISBN: 9789357696227

First edition 2022

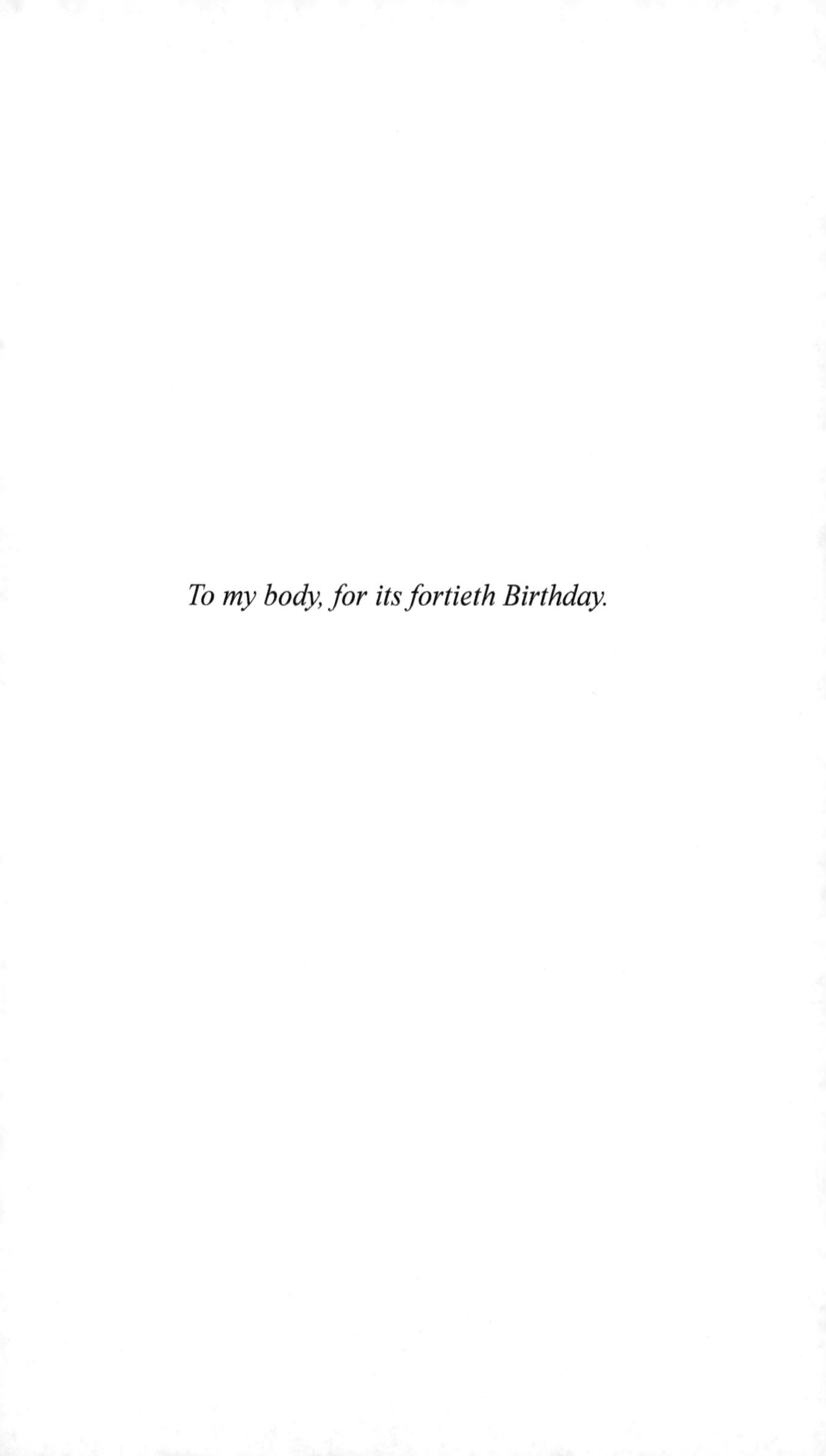

To my body, for its fortieth Birthday.

ACKNOWLEDGEMENT

I would like to thank my children and my husband for who they are, and my body for allowing me to reciprocate all the joy, care and love they give me. I love you.

1.

My body,
turns thirty eight years of life today.
It is my most unacknowledged loyal
friend.

Always here.
Always ready,
    For me.

Run!
Curl around that tree!
Climb up into the trunk of it.
Now, jump - Impress me!

Bravo,
It was almost a tie
With the resident winner in
        rope climbing,
Yet, it was the first time for you to touch it.
Bravo!
No, really, bravo - you surprised everyone
And yourself,
so much
that no one took the fact

about your strength seriously,
So we treated it like a one time event.

2.

What a strength!
Try some more of it.
Relocate the heavy stone from this land -
Make for others more space.

How considerate.
It's okey
hug your warmth not to escape.
Harder, don't let it go.

Hug.

Hug.

Don't cry,
now is not a good time.

Now,
Now is the time.
Cry yourself out.
Wake up crying.
Walk out trying.

3.

Feel,
feel the music,
Sway to it.

Lose yourself in the lyrics
of known and unknown songs
Hear the truth in them.
Relate.

Smile,
stretch,
caress.

A hangover?

Sweat it out!
You can do it.
Sustain.

Throw up all of the last night.
It's okey,
We will self hold our head.

Push the moron off of you!
Push him, let your adrenaline protect you.
We came only for the kissing.

Do a handstand.
A cartwheel.
Look, you are a star.

Second place in the race?
Well, GoodJob my friend.

Dance.
Dance like you just had discovered movement.

4.

6

Yes, you can lose it to him,
He is the one.
I approved, but
Ask him, wait
For him to agree too -
He is somebody's child, like you.

5.

Don't!
It's not a good moment to fart.

Girl, look at those legs you are
Pulling off in this dress.
You are amazing,
You are a star.

Jump in the water,
Feel it, as though you had been dirty your entire
life.

Step barefoot in the dunes
Of this desert.
Sink your soles
Drink some water.

6.

Say what now?
You are growing a person,
Here, inside?
Future mother - you are a star!

Yell: Labor should be taught at school!
    Twenty hours of pain,
    Write that down
    Pass it to school class.
Ask for gas.
Ask them to give you breath gas.
Natural Birth - by choice,
Oh là là !
I am telling you - You are a star.

Your breasts full with milky way
Spilling inside your little one,
Enjoy the time.

7.

You wonderful mother!
You did it again.
Trumpets proclaimed it.
Growing inside of you
Your second one.
One more galaxy forming inside.
But there are also faults in our stars.

You couldn't finish building this little one.

It's,
It's okay?
It's all right?
Is it?
I am not, are you?
Where would the milk go?

Look, knowing how many things need to be
there,
destined to click and fit into one another
So the nature could orchestrate
For the single act of conceiving.

Come,
We will cry.

Let's go to a therapy,
Let's hear how sadness sounds.
Hugs
Hugs
Hugs.

8.

Look, You run marathons now,
WOW.
A first,
Then a second one.

Shell we try to compose
Another human being to start growing
Inside of you?
I think it is a good time.
We have been grieving
For a long while -
Time is not on our side.

Oooooooh, it is an autoimmune disease
That is silently killing us.
I could had not hear you screaming:
No babies while I am under attack!

Really, self harming?
How typical this concept is for us.

9.

A hormonal therapy,
Yes,
I am so sorry I am doing this to you.
Buckle up,
Injection after injection
And fertilization.
Congratulations.
We are going to become a mother
For a second time.

Or is it a third one?
Who the hell defines life?

Twenty kilograms more, marks this pregnancy,
Write it down.
I cannot bend you
I cannot put you to sleep.

You want to be freezing in the room
Don't you?
It's okay, we will open the window,
On below zero,
We will sleep without the father next to us,

For no human should be boiling like that
Or to be freezing to death.

Come on,
Good morning,
Let's stand up now?
We will be happier when we clean out the house
For when the newborn arrives.
I know that's what you want too-
The feeling of the barefoot step
On an uncrumbed floor,
Imagine each of our step feet-kissing its
cleanliness.
Imagine,
Stand up now.
Could you please try?
Come on,
See,
You moved a bit.
Why are you not standing up?

10.

It is sad to learn we have parted ways.
You and me,
But you,
A force unstoppable.
I deeply apologize.
I have been taking you for granted
Neglecting you.
Leaving you to fight for our battles
Alone.

It's okay,
Don't sit up.
Lay down.
We will clean the house
Some other time.

This time
Around,
I hear you,
I see you,
How tired you are.

You are our master,
I obey you.
Do you want a pillow?

No, no, we are not standing up,
I would not make you do that.

I apologize, again, and will so hundreds more
times,
For I had taken you for granted
All these years have passed.

I am so sorry I have lost you - like a key
To enter my temple,
And had never gone
To search for you,
As though,
You were only the keychain,
And not the key itself.

NOw I saw that I had locked myself
Outside of you,
And that is the most terrifying thing.

Tell me,
Do you want to cry?
No?
It's okay,
Lay down, relax.
I won't bother you with thoughts.
Trust me,
Believe me -
Everything is as it should be.

I promise you an epidural with this pregnancy.
I promise that I would not torture you with
natural.
We know better this time,
Wherever we can, we will ask for help
From our science - friend.

11.

Good,
We arrived right on time for the epidural.
I am numb, but I observe the convulse
Distorting your roundness.
Tidal bulges of the
Amniotic fluid in the womb
Splashing the insides of the stomach,
There is no other way to go, than outside.

The things you endure,
The things you do for me,
You are a hero.

12.

Oh the waist…
Bones weeping
From every move
Muscles unwrapping
From bones
It hurts.

What have I done to you?
How does one lose weight when depressed?

Have to start running again,
Oh you marathon runner,
Half a kilometer is more than enough.
No need to be negotiating for more,
I know you are not strong on words, I know.
This time around you taught me to listen to you.
Through
The warmth you seep
Into the left nipple
For the little one to suckle
While he strokes
With his nails on your bare skin -
Offspring comes with claws,
But no mother would reveal

All the slits their babies
carve them with.
Yet, none of us weeps
As we know on the inside and the outside,
What it means to be weak.

I am not going to run struggling distances,
I learned the hard way,
And took me half,or a whole lifetime,
To peruse,
That you and I are not "one."
Feel the tenderness,
I droop to protect you
From how frail you had become.

13.

I felt milk-drop slide to the right nipple.
Really?
You are growing a baby again.
But I thought we will be barren till the end?

You are a miracle worker I must say.
A magician.
You make everything,
Out of nothing.

Thank you,
Thank you.
I'll keep you even safer this time,
The safest I ever had.

I'll nurture you,
While you nurture the baby in you.
We will be rearing our first daughter inside the
womb,
And our boys on the outside.
And I apologize for the noise
Oscillating around you,

We will be working in a kindergarten for a
while.
But I promise you a routine.
And not a particle of doing
Anything more than that.
Not a single gig,
Or an ambition to fulfill.

I would not chase
The need to feel accomplished -
I do not have a definition for it,
Anyways.

We would just rest, read, and
Nurse the humans you produced
By your own picture.
To inherit this world
So we could teach them
How to protect it.
As well as how to spark
The stardust.

14.

I love you,
You know I appreciate you,
I fulfilled my promise to be gentle to you,
I did not stuff you with unnecessary food,
We had a ten hours nightly sleep,
I kept us happy and at peace,
But could you please now
Make the contractions regular,
They do not admit us in the hospital?

We want an epidural again, remember.

I cannot stand the pain anymore.
What a powerful source you are.
Please make the contractions regular.

Aaaaand,
We are too late for epidural
This time around.
This is what happens when
Two parties do not listen

To one another
As you and I
Listen to each other.
I told them so many times,
That the baby is about to come out.

I am so sorry
I put you once again
Through natural birth giving.
I would tell them straight away
To give us gas to breathe
To relieve the pain.

Look at this nurse,
She smiles?
She thinks we are giving her
A thumbs up.
No nurse!
Raise up the gas,
Pump it up.

Why birth giving is such a loud event,
But silence predominates when
It is time for death?

Why am I asking such questions?

Body,
I think we are high.
Isn't is strange that there is somebody else
Inside of us?
You are like a matryoshka doll.

Look, she is coming out.

15.

I do not know how,
But I will make it up to us,
For everything
I had put you through
To survive.

16.

I thought it is a good idea
To indulge you into
A bite or few
Of cakes
Made to comfort you
When you wake up,
As I notice I am barely awake when you are
Breastfeeding the baby in the middle of the
night.

Now I see I had used you
As an excuse,
And I had parted further from
Where we were.

I had convinced myself - it is my body
That craves the cakes,
To anti-stress,
And I had piled unbearable weight.

And even further away
I had parted from you
When I forced you to exercise.
A tear was made,
I tore a ligament.

17.

The X-Ray glowed
And shone the cut I had inflicted -
A ghost with a broken spirit.

I guess I deserved the pain.
But you did not.

A ligament surgery is around
The corner for us.

I am sorry for the things
I had made you do.

In the silence of
Where I lie bedridden,
I feel you building up yourself,
And listen to
proteins negotiating between cells
For more
Density of the synovial fluid.
I hear you self-repair.

I kiss the laser mark
By bending the knee
Just a little bit.
You reproduce below the kiss
To protect me,
To serve me.

The damage I caused after all,
Turned out to be
For our own good:
By punishing one another,
We had found another way
To communicate.

I was blind to see
That you did not like weightlifting.

Running,
Running is the most joyful
Memory of the blessed life we had -
The closest distance we had run into one
another,
And had been together.
Balanced.

So,
We run in our dreams
And we wake up in sweat wondering:
"Would we be able to run ever again?"

18.

Did you hear the doctor?
Remarkable post surgical improvement
We had made.
Did all the resting,
And all the physiotherapy
To the point.
By December we will run again.
Smile, do you hear that?

I declare that we will not force ourselves,
And we will always
Carefully self-regulate.

This is a second chance,
And with it I want to celebrate You.

19.

This is a second chance,
And with it I want to celebrate You.

Could I write about you?
Give me a sign?
Yes.
Thank you.

20.

My body turns thirty eight today.

This year I will respect it.
I owe it to it.

We do not owe to anyone
As much as we owe
To our body. Yet,
We ignore it.
We live with the pretense
That we control it
Or it controls us.
But it is a balance.
It has to be mutual care
And understanding.

This year I single my wish to "losing weight,"
I'll mend to my body
And listen to it.
Will meditate.
Will love it.

It is a general wish -
I know,
As common as the one

From kids for an iPhone
Or an Xbox.
But I do not wish it for appearance, or
As a consumer to consume it.
I wish it for a future with minimized pain
I wish it as an obedience and
gratefulness.

21

My dearest body,
Thank you.
You are to me,
And I am to you,
Your most loyal friend.
I'll do everything possible,
To not forget even for a minute
That.